WOMEN
WHO DREAM TIGERS

WOMEN WHO DREAM TIGERS

VICKI SUMMERFELDT

THISTLEDOWN PRESS LTD.

©1997, Vicki Summerfeldt
All rights reserved

No part of this publication may be reproduced or transmitted in any form or by any means, electronic or mechanical, including photocopying, recording, or any information storage and retrieval system, without permission in writing from the publisher.

Canadian Cataloguing in Publication Data
Summerfeldt, Vicki, 1954 –
Women who dream tigers
(New leaf editions)
ISBN 1-895449-76-6
I. Title. II. Series.
PS8587.U486 W65 1997   C811'.54   C97-920163-2
PR9199.3.S858 W65 1997

Book design by A.M. Forrie
Set in 12 pt. Jenson
by Thistledown Press Ltd.

Printed and bound in Canada by
Veilleux Impression à Demande
Boucherville, Quebec

Thistledown Press Ltd.
633 Main Street
Saskatoon, Saskatchewan
S7H 0J8

THE CANADA COUNCIL | LE CONSEIL DES ARTS
FOR THE ARTS | DU CANADA
SINCE 1957 | DEPUIS 1957

We acknowledge the support of the Canada Council for the Arts for our publishing program. Thistledown Press also gratefully acknowledges the continued support of the Saskatchewan Arts Board.

ACKNOWLEDGEMENTS:

The poem "Interlude" appeared in *Harvest Magazine* and "i turn back to her holding" appeared in *Grain*.

The author sends thanks to Glen Sorestad for offering editorial assistance. To Jill Carroll, much gratitude for her unfailingly sharp intellect, her visionary perception, her mastery with the editor's pen and her willingness to splurge for supper. To Scott, blessings for the time before time. And to two special women who dream dragons into life, Beth Summerfeldt and Joan Hiltz.

CONTENTS

Women Who Dream Tigers 9
Cockfighting 10
Prairie Spring 11
Contemplation of a River Suicide 12
She Found Christ 13
For All the Marys 14
Between Bites 15
Lavender Jane 16
Sisters 17
Pathos 18
Fine Lines 19
Old Age 20
Meetings 21
Visitor 22
Car Rebel 23
Holiday 24
Moving Away 25
The Day You Left 26
Beginning 27
Harvest 28
It Had Been a Dusty Day 29
Auguries 30
Reunion 31
Adultery 32
Conversation with a Sleeping Husband 33
Repainting the Day 34
Lover Past 35
Birthday 36
After Work 37

Funeral   38
Lunch   39
Nanny   40
Interlude   41
Tea Time   42
I.C.U.   43
Close Friend   44
Golden Oldies   45
Hallowed Death   46
Dale   47
Snake Eyes   48
After the Reading   49
Voodoo   50
Paper Art   51
Pagan Prayer   52
Coming of Merlin   53
Saturday Morning   54
Isolation   55
An Intimate Moment   56
Kirk   57
It Was the Rain That Sealed Us In   58
Writing   59
Voices   60
Life Swell   61
Prufrock   62
My Love Is Come to Me   63
i turn back to her holding   64

WOMEN WHO DREAM TIGERS

she rubs her eyes
and smooths the small creases
of surprise
from her skin

today she realized
in one swift twist
that her tenuous filaments
of self to dreams
were nothing but air

dry desert   empty   dead

but wait
if she presses her face
into blanched dreamscape
ignores the skeletal remains
of hopes that have fallen
she sees herself   a sleek tiger
rippling over sand   dangerous
in her quest for water and tall grass
a predator who drinks arterial blood
and thrives

the tiger   eyes guiltless
drowses and becomes a warm silhouette
in the setting sun
her body twitches and sleep rolls in
as the tiger fierce
dreams of breathing fire
and knows that the glittering magic
of dragons and earth caves
is nothing but air

COCKFIGHTING

Themistocles stopped his Greek army
to watch two fighting cocks
demanded that his dusty soldiers
like the cock warriors
fight with a stubborn will

they did
and conquered the Persians

Athens elevated the warring cocks
to the gods
lavished on them
the splendours of victory

and the Greek taste for cock
spread across the lands

heated faces rolled bets
at pit sides
egging on the birds
frenzied by iron spurs
and savage stimulants

this brutal art
cocking for royal diversion
cut wings at a slope
shortened the fan of tail feathers
pruned the fleshy comb
to a slight smear of colour on the crown

kill   small warhorses
your quills red
with blood

PRAIRIE SPRING

you can see it now
subtle shades of green
just under the dry crust
of brown leaves rotted away by winter
and the air smells different
full of sweet stirrings
beyond the window

a man in a blue jacket and ball cap
crawls out of his truck
stretches long into the sun
smiles at the kid on a bike
pedalling with steamy frenzy past him

he takes off his coat
tosses the crumpled roll
back into the truck
and before he knows what he's doing
opens his arms
face creased into a mirrored ball of sun
spins wildly in a circle
laughter painting delicious colour
on side street silence

the dizzy fall on a neighbour's lawn
sobers him
he remembers adult dignity
stands up
wipes dry twigs from his shoulders
and walks into his house
followed by the soft echo
of double dare summers

CONTEMPLATION OF A RIVER SUICIDE

arms crossed over each other
a warm nest for a head
made hazy and weighted by
the sadness
that could not be shaken

fingers spread open
and run tentatively
through the grass of unwashed hair
then touch the face
that had lost itself
in the great pain of the world
so sharp in its glare
that eyes remain closed

it was later in the pain
when the kiss
of a starred lizard
born of a will to live
frightened the inner eyes open
to look at her own death

her belly convulsed flat
against the earth
the snap of sharp stems
and twigs cutting life
into her

she sat up
away from the cradle of her
own sour smell
staggered weakly into the rain

SHE FOUND CHRIST

on a Sunday morning in McDonald's
the sun glinted off
a freshly wiped Formica table top
and the remaining streaks of water
shimmered with celestial promise

the restaurant almost empty
purled with the soft discussion
of workers as they wadded napkins
into metal holders
and sprayed plastic surfaces clean

in a pocket of quiet
a beam of morning light
shone through the side window
hit her so hard she squinted
covered her eyes
felt the sacred breath on her skin

she recalls it so vividly
it has her shaking
a voice spoke
(some say the radio she claims divine)
deep   masculine   and reassuring

he calmed her with his words
promised revelation   transformation
and life forevermore

that's why she sits here now
at a back table on Sunday morning
she waits for divinity
with her coffee and muffin

FOR ALL THE MARYS

she had a long streak of a face
smudged sullen by a life
where nothing came easy
and even the happy times
were gnawed at
by a vague nomadic anxiety

nothing fresh belonged to her
life in a side mirror
sharp with detail
that she was just beyond reaching
the action always going on behind
as she sped away
from the curved reflection
of other people's pleasure

the quick glint
of light on surface
left her knowing
a half beat off
that she was empty

nobody took the time
to lay a hand upon her face
let the hollows fill
with a tender swell
of murmured concern
and she shy sad woman
with calloused hands
that smelled of toilet water
didn't have the courage
to reach out

BETWEEN BITES

garlic bundles dangle from roof beams
absorb the clatter of dishes
and swishing conversations

they sit neatly in the centre
of the restaurant
she wears a white sweater over pink
bits of coral caught in the crease of her neck
delicately
dips into a cool swirl
of ice cream and whipped topping

watches carefully
between bites
the man who sits beside her
grey sweater grey hair grey face
bent over
nose nearly touching his dish

it is painful
slow   slow
so old
the move from food to mouth

her face
white as the purse hanging from her chair
catches his shame
and with straight backed dignity
wipes his mouth
quickly
without disturbing
the movement
of spoon into mouth

LAVENDER JANE

It's a woman's colour
reminiscent of sharp
edged purple
only prettier
margins smudged into a lip
sticked mouth
fresh kissed

smell gardens
lilac laden
pastel watercolours
of old women
artificial hint of youth in
grey hair mouths the colour of bruise
healing beneath the skin
eyes circled by the soft lustre
of plum
necks violet scented
soft rouged cheeks
tasting of time gone
a room where a
clear raisin tinted bottle
of cologne
caught in sunlight
on a dresser
where a clock
makes the only sound

SISTERS

that night he said in the soft dust of love
you are beautiful   I am
opened where I have been closed

she let the hair fall over her face   turned away
unbelieving that this lover had shifted around
to welcome a stranger
it didn't matter   lovers lied

later she would stare for hours
into her own eyes not as dark as they once were
and hear the echo of her father
feel the pinch on white cheek with one hand
while he twisted her arm with the other

on good days she rode high the princess his princess
but when she had displeased him
he would call her squaw face   slut   and laugh
she knew the spill of shame should not exist
but the caress of blonde hair on rose blush
meant nothing without obedience
and when she decorated her face with paint
wore warrior jeans that worked devilishly
around her hips smoked Export A with no filter
and guzzled beer
she knew she had been knocked from the pedestal
with a dusty thump into a world of bad girls
who drank and fucked and had many babies

she would watch them through the smoke
hear the sneer in the voice of her white father
knew that to be woman was to be tried
and found guilty no matter the colour

PATHOS

with his gardener mouth
he cut
and snipped
her blooms
until everything
dried up
and she blew
like a tumbleweed
across the bleak desert
of home

later
under the covers of night
he expected
lush response
thinking it was
simply the wet from his kiss
that was needed
to bring her back into leaf
turn grey
into florid bush

she would hold him
dutifully
dry twigs snapped
by the blinding grind of his dust storm

gritty and powerful
he blew her tumbleweed self
away

FINE LINES

they say
as we get older women dry up
our breasts grow useless
flattened by grasping
mouths pulling for milk
and sexual succour

our skin ridged and loose waits
under hands folded patient
over stretch marked bellies

we force the passion passive
our deep well dried up   they say
the need to rub wild
on the skin of another
fall into the bliss of a kiss
gone

don't believe
that the years we held
the babies needy
the men broken
the women soft rounded
are forgotten

don't believe
we don't need anymore
because we grow old
and should be content
with dreams and memories
that whistle by on a passing thought

old skin still craves soft touch
the clutch of life holding onto life

OLD AGE

I lean back behind the steering wheel
feel warm sun stretch over me
my fingers tap some aimless tune
that passes through my mind
without sticking
what should I say in class about getting old
how can the just ripened
possibly imagine?
even I   on the brink
of lined skin and grey hair
have trouble capturing the shape
of nodding old age

with the sleepy sideways glance
of a fat cat I notice
in the car that slides alongside
an old man perched
regal on the red seats
of his white chariot

I squint and imagine him young
erase the lines   the wattles
let the rim of age
fall from his face to see
the knight of ages past
dapper on his milky steed
noble in spite of the bent
shoulders and cloudy eyes
I bet he still stirs the heart
of a damsel
whose greying hair
falls on rouge rose cheeks
as she bends to him

MEETINGS

there's a world
sun scrunched shadows on leaves
leaves curled red and orange
just out through the window

a magpie plays a game
up and down
on the edge of the grass
defiantly flicking her freedom
at us
on the inside
in the inside of a room
listening
without hearing the words from the front
ignoring
the blur of black words
on white screen
eyes drawn instead
to the black trace
of a bird
writing escape
on a wing

VISITOR

clickety clang clang clickity clang clang
you clatter and bang pots and pans
beggar into my neighbourhood
onto my step
and the rubadub shine
of your face
warped round in the metal curve
of the cooking wares
looks expectant
as I open the door

in goes your foot
then that large nose of yours
sniffs around corners
smelling what I've been doing
and with who and when
and be damned if I don't
tell you snake oil woman
slithering in with the shimmer
of dented metal
and knives sharpened
by the flinty hone of your tongue
you pull a soap job on me
and I am left blowing bubbles
as your cart pulls out of sight

I am uneasy
vaguely aware of being danced over
then abandoned with a medicine bottle
filled with nothing
but wormwood

CAR REBEL

it was the slash of sun
across the shadowed seat
of my early morning drive
that incited
my rebellion
against a day inside
straight walls
and straight rules
slicing minutes
into purpose

so here we are now
students
and teacher
perched on hills growing yellow
in autumn breath

they murmur
or sit quietly
allow the cool kiss
of September
to brush against their faces
the school more friendly
from over here
where we sit
in the company
of curling breezes
and warm earth

HOLIDAY

brown eyed susans
by the side of the road
wave us out
like a golden chain
of smiles
on a promising neck

they are a succulence
in a ridge
of parched grass

dancing girls
painted gaudy
decadence
on a monochromatic plain flatland

thanks for the send off dollies
but
I can't say
I'll miss you

MOVING AWAY

my life
is a closed room
and I dream
of wind
dancing erratic through my bones
around my spine
tumbling me
into freedom

the paisley froth
of white foam
and hazy sunset
embroider my skin

the gale stops
and when I hit ground
I will roll
break the fall
with a roll
become tangled
in dry leaves
and sharp twigs

but I will pull out the thorns
wipe off the dirt
blow leaves away
and walk into
another wind

THE DAY YOU LEFT

the mean spirited wind today
hurls hapless snow
from the roof
just beyond my window

I watch crystal beauty
   small
   helpless
   tossed
scramble wildly
to stay afloat
one last futile attempt
before the anonymous meld
into a five foot snowbank

and I curl down
into the warm nest
of blue blanket
look out at the storm
to quell the one
that ices up my middle
and I know too late
that I've been taken
by the wind
my strength nothing against the tempest
that pushes and presses
and knocks me down
under my covers

clothes scratch rough on raw desire
and I close my eyes to the storm
bend my face into the pillow
and try to keep breathing

BEGINNING

the shaded blessing of dusk
smudges the small room

plants press black spindly patterns
through the remaining window light
as I sit naked on your floor

you are somewhere behind me
close enough to touch
but not
close

and I can't unravel myself
from the choking panic
that somewhere along the way
we should have stopped
before one of us
could do any harm

you kiss my spine
pull me down
to the promise
of sweet tenderness
and no pain

but the dark has settled
and there is a chill
in the air

HARVEST

there was a field
    that sang a lullaby
of yellow grain
soft clapping hands
    in the wind
    and warm sun

you took me there
    to lay me down
        on the cushion of earth
        and sky reflections

took me there
    with a passion
        true
to ardent beginnings

and it was there
in the vast embrace
of prairie
that we tasted
each other
soft down
in the gully
of a farmer's field

IT HAD BEEN A DUSTY DAY

Every face was grey and pinched
disinterested eyes nested in hollows of shadow
spirits trampled by the ashen wash of
    no green on the trees
    no rainbows luring children
    the ugly nowhere land
    between winter and spring
As I struggled with bags
the daily burden of papers and books
the sun caught me in the parking lot
the sky opened into a wide gold capped smile
    I could smell a childhood pasture
    taste the delicious tang of a cow's salt lick
    see that neighbourhood redhead
    who always drank water from rusted cans
    got suddenly sticky with the
    warm spin of hide 'n seek games
    on a late night in my old back alley
up one side   swish   the child ran
almost knocking my stolid self sideways
down the other   plunk   landing with both feet
in the sweet simplicity of a land
where a stolen kiss from a runny nosed boy
was ecstasy
and we would all be best friends
blood to blood until we died

The sky shut its mouth then
closed off the skipping dreams
and sandalwood smell of summer night pleasure
I started to walk   still carrying
the same bags and papers and books
precious now   made golden magic
by the soft light of possibility

AUGURIES

the soft hush of early morning
muted the sounds the two of us made
dancing our hurried steps
of getting ready for the day

a thud on the window
drew my daughter's attention
away from cereal
made her jump up from the table
to look out at the stunned bird
bent and awkward on the ground
still dazed by the deception
of glass

let's save the bird she cried
bring her inside
safe from cats
and the like

I said   no
to cage even the injured
would be wrong
leave her   she'll find her way

reluctant my child followed
footsteps slow
knowing I lied

and all day
I couldn't shake the fear
that someone
other than the bird
would die

REUNION

girl   you've grown
into a grandmother
and I can't stop
lifting your ten year old face
out of the one
that now looks at me
talks at me
from across the table

the problem is
that your hair
has gone grey
some strange jester
is at work

the sharp angles and alert eyes
lost
roundness of age
circles your face

the same number of years
are notched into our belts
and I am surprised
that you had the courage
to coddle
this fat folded image of comfort
instead of smoking and swearing
your way   razor edged and rebellious
into a new dimension riddled with challenge
instead of this huddled fear
in a shadowed corner
of growing old

ADULTERY

you came
to me last night
dark cloaked in the mystery
of elusive moon
and dream

I rolled across
the smooth coolness
of my own sheets
onto the rough
and unfamiliar cloth
of you

the safe dream shimmer
became an abrasive scrape
and nipped me aware
to how much
I wanted to dip
into that cookie jar
lick sweet crumbs
smack down
as much as I could
before getting myself slapped
by daylight

CONVERSATION WITH A SLEEPING HUSBAND

In night's centre   I let my clothes fall off   allowing for the sudden evaporation of evening scent   I lean over   scoop them up from the floor   and for a moment I hold them to my face   spin back into the dark of smoke and dancing smell of where I've been   I drop them again and stretch naked into the cold air   pad across the shadow streaked hallway into the bedroom   quietly alive with his shallow breathing   I slip into bed smoothly   not once disturbing the rhythm of his deep sleep   waves that ripple into dream ocean   It's not hard to slide cross current and move in along his back   strong and wide   I curl into the familiar lines   wedge a cold leg into his   push my arm through his and around the expanse of bare chest   Safe at last   away from the chaos of elsewhere and runaway thoughts that scrape at the glaze of my comfort

Even in sleep he knows I am there   rolls over on his back and allows me to crawl tighter into him   my face resting on the sweet matted hair   I breathe in the clean smell of soap and silent warmth

Let it be only you   just you   second skin to my skin   just you   and I kiss the chest   breathe deep again into his standstill swell of calm and my nervous sense of not resting easy with myself begins to steady with his breathing   His hand over mine and I breathe   in again   our gain safe   Come sleep   close my eyes to the deep soft sleep of husband and wife

REPAINTING THE DAY

dreary old day
steel against the grey sag of sky
pressing me
into a melancholy mist
until the elfin kiss
of your gossamer wings
fluttered along my face
and lured my dancing spirit
into a circle where I spun
elegant magic
in stardust and mouseweb

good companion
you tossed me the gold coin
led me out to the rainbow
and said
lift your face
let the colours run into the breath of you
paint the landscape of heart
push blood into life
pulse love
and become the silk thread
woven into the sifting sigh
of life

my grey day became buoyant
with diamond dust
and puckish kiss

LOVER PAST

it was out of the corner of my eye
that I saw the familiar shape of you
the stark line of hair and shoulder
the laughing throw back of face

it's been a while I thought
and felt nothing not even shame
at how shamelessly I loved you

the absurd clench of memory
clutched for only a breath
and was gone

I knew that you had seen me
out of the corner of your eye
did you think I still cared?
and it became important to let you know
how little it all meant
a soft wind
maybe we should have coffee
and I could pour out in cupfuls
and sugar spoons
how you were nothing
except imagination

instead I pretend to just miss seeing you
and focus on the point just beyond where you stand

you did the same
as we walked aloof and uncaring
in opposite directions

BIRTHDAY

you just yawned
and told me how tired you get now
how it's hard to stay up
past ten

you've forgotten when we put
the bottles on the table
emptied them of their hot blood
filled our veins
with wild talk

without meaning to
we loved each other's promise
to become more than ordinary
and we would splash wine
into the dreams
fall into believing
that nothing would end the pleasure
of being an audience
for each other

it was you   remember
who taught me how to belly dance
to Bob Dylan
vowed to become
a painter a dancer a poet

and tonight
you are 40
ready for sleep
before the cork is out
of the bottle

AFTER WORK

just fell into the
cold belly of a car
alone from early morning
the key turns
stiff and irascible
I push up my head
listen to the sullen heater squeal
protest this sharp kick in the side
after a sleepy hideaway day
in a parking lot

I bounce and twitch
to warm away the blast
of gelid air
and ragged impressions
fresh from the classroom
crammed with the constant
grind of ego and demand
nattering
like this old car mutters at me
thunka thunka chunk chunk
go away day
thunka thunka
let's go away
into night
with a smooth ride home
no radio
or winter crazed drivers
just the cold
and a car
that warms up
under my touch

FUNERAL

I'm grateful for her
the winter moon
full belly hanging ripe
pushing against the dark
I'm driving into
the night black
just beyond the touch
of pale beams
night
made blacker by your going

eulogized
your life your death was
velvet painted
into Rockwell sweetness
dusty sleep
made magic and tranquil

and I wonder
if you felt comforted
by the muted whisper
of your own ending

I'd rather you were here
pierced by the white edges
of a full-mooned night

LUNCH

Sweat broke out
on my upper lip
the last time
I rolled my tongue over
your cayenne skin
and the heat
tumbled down my centre
erupting into
a taste fiesta

these snow blanketed days
need the jalapeño
bite of your kiss
to melt me into
a golden siesta

meet me
on a blanket

we'll make it our beach

you bring the nachos
I'll wear a sombrero

we'll make castanets
dance

NANNY

they've said it for years now
the men in the family
that I'm like you

every time my voice rises in anger
or I take offense at being quieted
I am accused of getting more like you
crazy spinaround grandmother
who at 80 drives wild down maritime backroads
dirt and dust flying
towards a lover
20 years younger

any time I refuse to bend
into a laugh-behind-hand kind of woman
I am you
lone mad woman
housed in rooms warmed by stacked folds
of thrift bargain clothing
boxes of paper and bottles
and tea cups from children
you taught

you keep them around you
like friends
grandmother
that I'm like

INTERLUDE

just stepped from the shower
a sacrificial scrubbing of soil
from skin rubbed repentant
by exotic coral   deep sea echoes
of ceremonial cleansing

you sit
on the toilet   lid closed
simply watching

even though years
have packed on weight
between us and my pale skin
boasts no claim to beauty
you smile   eyes approving
and suddenly I cross
arm over breasts
reach for a towel
a modest reaction
to your interest

just now I am not
the rough tumbledown woman
of every morning light
you watched
splayed and awkward
in birth giving
or vomiting bad fish
on a New Hampshire roadside

I am new right now
years evaporated
in the hot steam

TEA TIME

I watch city gardeners
two women young & brown baked
root in the spring soil
squat in sweaty glory
over the earth
its rich dark softness
eager to be planted
to feel the suckle of roots
at its granular teat

I watch spring move
into summer
envy the muscle stretch
and sweat trickle of the two
even consider in passing
getting up off the bench
to move
into the warm day's arms
and become an active partner

but a silken purr
of sunbeam warms me
and keeps me sitting
smiling with thoughts
of sunflowers
and tea in English gardens

I.C.U.

my hands are dry
cracked from the ritual
of wash and dry purging
that must be done before touching you
white against pale pillow
looking small and fragile
delicate soft contrast
to the hard edge of machines
feeding you
with a soft hum beep and drip
of technical life electrical blood
force fed through you
to keep you with us
on this side of life

there is silence here
an awed respect for life
near its end
we pace dustless corridors
back and forth
frantic fear under control
nurse voices tumble low
trying not to let us know
how immune they are
to our suffering

can you feel the breath
of our helplessness
brush your cold cheek
when we smile and kiss murmurs of
good health and sour fear
against your ear?

CLOSE FRIEND

she asked me about you tonight
in that linear unlined way of the young
wondered if in another time
beyond this place of
my husband   your wife
and the children in between
we would have loved each other
more than
and different from right now

the question was answered with slick speed
no rupture of hesitation
we are friends no matter what slot in time we fill
but as I drove into the delicious darkness
I skipped over reality for a minute
saw myself slip beside you
to cradle you and kiss

my imaginings drew back
ashamed that even in this fabricated landscape
of just suppose
my mouth should have rested on yours
hands molding fingers against the curve of your head
into the sweet smell of hair
curl matted by stroking

it's just a never should

but my friend
I'll never sit as easy over coffee
knowing that when you weren't looking
we loved each other for
a little while

GOLDEN OLDIES

the song broke out of the radio
in a radiant burst
of strobe lights
and dope smoke
magic carpet ride
pumping through the corridors
of my middle class life
a tranquil day
hit full force
with a swat from long ago
a drunken hazy time
when my young mouth
was lipsticked white
and black painted eyes looked
artificially surprised
at everything we did
and I wiggled and swizzled my way
through a world I wasn't ready for
would watch
through the strands of ironed hair
the irony of my own existence
boys fed me vodka straight
desperate to touch my breasts
and I let myself believe
they were falling in love with me

by the time the song is done
I am glad
to be over forty
and forgetful

HALLOWED DEATH

like the shadowed evil
of old black and whites
they huddle beside the casket
a small crowd in mourning colours
crying out against
the frozen glint of snow
and the sudden recognition
of death

they form a dark blot
on the bleak white countryside
closed in on each other
for protection against early winter

the witches murmur through brittle trees

I turn half expecting
the swoop of bat or the curling steam
of some vile cauldron promising
life beyond body to earth

on Hallowe'en day
my hands   pushed deep in pockets
are beginning to claw curl
from the cold
I mourn for the life that is gone
for the going of my own

I close my eyes
let the aggressive nip
of October goblins
anger me to fight the panic
of oak and metal
lowered to the grave

DALE

It was a pungent combination of things that put you in mind today   the radio played an old song by Creedence that you sang off key at every party   Then there was the sky   a glorious Saskatchewan sky   slate blue and rich with not just ordinary clouds   but prairie clouds that embroidered the hem of infinity   God could reach out and touch the grey edge

It could have been the musty hint of thaw   you know how earth smells are   Anyway   today   even with the snow   it was warm enough to go without a coat   I could swill and swallow air without a cold thorn piercing my breath   and felt that young listen to loud music kind of joy   That's why I felt you here   loving you years after your death   I get to see the season   not have it seep through me

I leave the house   afraid to remember   this walk by the side of a bootleg spring gets me thinking your face   inventing you now with lines   hair grey   a shadowy vignette that startles me   You would have been beautiful

A bird's litany skims above the traffic and I hold still for the prayer in this sad still time   The wind   an abrupt heave of winter   sends me into a spiral backslide home   leaving me with an impish wisp of your lips on my cheek

SNAKE EYES

took some doing to work myself free of you
scratching off the snake skin
transparent sinew corkscrewed
into my marbled arteries
can't say you broke my heart
that black old thing chewed off at the edges
but mistrust made an encore
slithered in again
I was stupid to believe that meandering smile
I knew you   I thought
knew what you'd do

I didn't
life always seems to do that
just when I start to have faith

you'd think I would know by now
but I was crushed
by hypnotic anaconda eyes
and flickering words

AFTER THE READING

later I
tried to crawl out of your story
(lyrical woman voice singing rape)
by pounding myself with the grind
of music   annie lennox raging   loud in the car

and I drew blood
prying apart the swamp weeds around my throat
that pull me backwards through myself

to when   the times   can't forget
he took me   child   to the attic for comics

my eyes
   swallowing coloured print
his hand
   moving my girl hand
   to limp damp crotch

return the favour
he said
I did
and hurt yet
   from the fingers pushing
   and aborted penetrations
   of a man
   into a girl body too small

tonight
   I was punched back to the attic
   where I never wanted to go again

never a child again

VOODOO

there's deviltry afoot
these nights that squat low-lying
on me
you stretch across my mind
but I want to bend away
not into you

I need an amulet
    a star kissed talisman
    a fetish for my fetish
so I search the dark
    alleys under stones
      into the bowels of magic
      burning powerful

come shaman   chant a ritual rune
pagan women
dance me into the healing centre
    of myself
Merlin promises to conjure
a sideshow brilliant enough
    to erase you
just to be safe
give me a warlock
on a marble slab
or the pious creed
of a priest in black

any sorcery
to exorcise you
from the night

PAPER ART

I want to sketch you
> with words

use full/ripe idiom
> to unveil

the soft warmth of your mouth
the sweet slide of your tongue
> on me

I will
> cull fine etchings
> from you

scatter
them on my canvas
> iridescent

with your design

PAGAN PRAYER

just beyond
that curving hill
the glory of paradise
was visited upon me

there had been sleep
before the golden rain
of fingertips
worshipped my skin

I arched back
over the cool altar
smelling of ancient faith
and when the tongue spread my lips
I grew pliant
and reverential
in the moist venerable press
of you

there is a glint of reborn morning

faith
keep the faith

solemn and naked
I bend in prayer
while you kiss my back
and whisper
praise be

COMING OF MERLIN

they knew   mother and father
warmed me in the hearth fire
but warned me against the incantations
of men who were not men
and my confessor held both my hands
read into my eyes pious platitudes
reminded me in each prayer that the stranger was waiting
to scorch me with his heat and leave me pulsing with child
I listened well and heeded their lessons until
the sprinkle of morning light took me from my bed
lured me to the hillside
so delicious was the sun through leaves
that I shed my gown and pressed my back against the grass
unguarded   I spread myself open
and he came in a strong wind
devil nails scratching to hold me compliant while he
filled me again and again
with molten lava
burning scars to my womb
where Merlin would live

later my confessor held me
allowed the church to claim the child
because I was taken by no man
and the magic of the child
needed goodness on its side

he fell from me with a sparkle and a twist
and I knew
even though he now belonged to the god of white light
that the child tugging furiously at my breast
looked at me
with the eyes of his father

SATURDAY MORNING

sweet pleasure this
running my legs
bare against sheets
the long stretch of body in bed
I slide down roll round and press
my face in the smell of last night
and centuries of bed history

I will stay here all day
morning thoughts
weep out from this timeless rumple
of body on mattress under covers
that holds the warm scent of my body
and mind
making maze of image upon image

I love being in bed
let my hand mess my hair
wild and upright
drink the warm milky coffee
and read the nonsense
of mad scribbles
scribble the mad nonsense
of writers in bed
wiggle comfortably down
in the down of a quilty hug
and stay in my warm bed
I'll stay where dreams play
let the busy condemn me
I'll stay in my bed
yes I will
stay all day
in my bed

ISOLATION

the only sound
I have allowed in
is the uneven staccato
of an Ikea clock
7 bucks max and noisy

the phone is on holiday
like everyone else
except me

I am at home
a hermit
holed up in a bed
covered with books
dreaming
of vermilion plumage
and reeds on thatched huts
wet from the soundless tears
of rats
surprised by a snake's jaws

brick red spots on black and yellow scales
colour death

my legs kick
just before I'm swallowed
by the bright shock
of spontaneous generation
from putrid matter

it reminds me of why
I like to be alone

AN INTIMATE MOMENT

it's been a while
since I spread my fingers
over the smooth
white virtue
of paper silk skin

let the sultry musk
of between sheets air
billow soft words
sighing to be
burnished by the hot force
of pen

my hands
open over the pages
rest lightly
on the clean surface
caress the unmarked margins
enjoy the frosty
response
of an indifferent lover
who looks coyly over one shoulder

but as I reach for the pen
the coquettish paper
uncurls with a pleasure blush
pretending
that all along
it had been waiting
for my stroke

KIRK

there was the confusing blur
of sound smearing into coloured
teeshirts   matted hair and the
sour smell of confined animals
ready to break loose
from the school

I nearly lost ground
but the wave after wave was broken
by the low voice
of a boy with a poem
beside me
folded paper held out

quick words
about a girl
stroked alive like a painting

I read aloud
and watched his face plump up
with the artistic brush
of pink flush
eyes lit with the renaissance gold
of sacred on canvas
as he blended into art

hair covered one eye
and he become a sketch
of frailty and passion
the thin fibres of
his life to love
held in my reading

IT WAS THE RAIN THAT SEALED US IN

sheets of cold August rain
kept us at the kitchen table
and I suppose
it was that forced intimacy
that made you ask me
to read a poem

and fooled by the mesmerizing lull
of an early furnace
dark clouds
and hot coffee
I did

after it was over
you said it was too hard to understand
could I explain

so I tried
and you replied it is open
to a hundred interpretations
and I sputtered yes
that is good
and you said no
it is too complex

so I run a desperate poet
seeking love and approval
I find a simple poem
read it
and you say how stupid
any fool could have written that

WRITING

is like that silent moment
just after
in the tumble of sweated up sheets
when skin is flushed and mottled
with rubbing ourselves against
each other

it's in that quiet afterglow
that I must
with sullen need
crawl into the covers
nuzzle sated self into self

go away   leave me   I'm done with you

it's like a poem that itches to get put down
with the urgency of labial swell
needing to be rubbed
back and forth across paper
until it shudders out
slack mouthed with the moment
and falls hapless on the paper

then comes that candescence
the sweet emission on paper

I finger its loveliness
still tender
then turn away a little ashamed
by the wanton expression

depleted by the
squeeze of words pressed from me

VOICES

the Yeats woman said
while angling her porcelain doll head
to face me
that she didn't write poetry because
there were no voices speaking inside of her head
don't you hear them?

I pull away suddenly guilty
because someone knows about you
how on better days
you are simply a seductive whisper
that teases with barely heard words
then usually late at night
comes the laughing babble
of too many friends for dinner
voices jumbled and confusing
I grow weary of this banter
and crawl away to sleep
until forced awake
by the echo of your voice
hitting itself against my skull
making itself known
demanding to be translated
into silk thread ink on paper

I suppose I do hear something
I say stiff and shifty eyed
as though telling would break the spell
and angered by my treachery
you might grow mute
refuse to visit me anymore
leave me sullen and empty
of the words to say how empty I am

Margaret surfaced and wrote out her pain about childbirth and how she would never again allow them the hollow eyed spectres of hospital hallways   to punctuate her natural rhythm with needles and straps and military invasions into a non violent zone   no more babies she said   never again no more babies for her   she is right of course about powerlessness and the lethal intent of medical control over human substance   they are afraid of birth and stand back nervously and see with suspicion the waves of a woman's abdomen rippling down with an earthbound pull primitive gravity calling to its newborn beyond masked faces and the metal rattle of beds with wheels eyes dead from too much death these technicians of illness cannot fathom the primal tide that rolls back and forth   back and forth   constant and regular a beautiful sea whose surging swell brings life to land

there is no escaping
your dismal sense of worthlessness
as you wend your way through the poem
balding man with worn elbows
and frayed edges
tired of the skipping stone banter
of daily intercourse
and with every sad sour realization
you shrink
until your pants are rolled up against thin ankles
and you grow old but still love
teaspoons and mermaids and fog purring to life

there has been rain here
on this brown prairie
the cold and hot
mix wet into an opalescent haze
that slides over the flats
trailing snail ooze across fields
and on city streets
misted fingers hang on to building edges
and window ledges
an ominous damp works itself into me
and the fog pins me to questions
that are dry of answers
I feel my hair growing thin
my life trim and measured
with you on my arm
I then bend weary and stiff
roll my pants up
and go off to listen
to women
in rooms

"... MY LOVE IS COME TO ME"
(from "Birthday" by Christina Rossetti)

from under my lamp in a night shadowed room
she pulled herself up out of the page
shook a hundred years' rest
from her golden brow
and faced me
so close
I saw the rose on her cheeks

breathe soft into my heartblood
Christina
veiled magic
brings you across time
your fine fingers   still wet with ink
opened a space through centuries
clouded by powder bone and
pulverized by mortality

you escaped through these words
these poems that I wrap myself in

suddenly it is not the language
that holds me
it is you
your laughing life
spilling over into mine
tender lips
whetting a warm heat in me
as murmured poesy
slides down
my throat
and into my heart

I TURN BACK TO HER HOLDING
(for Susan Andrews Grace)

let me ask   i ask the woman across the table   hair a whorled bonnet around her face   exhaustless spirals that coil into comfort   she makes it safe to say susan   i'm confused   can you tell me what is a prose poem   exactly?   there is no exactly in a poem of prose   she answers   it is a feel   a running your fingers down over the words   and creating from straight lines a glyphic lace of image   i see   thank you   blind   i pick up the pencil/chisel   eye the marble square of ordinary words   edges blunt   like an unimaginative lover   where should it begin   the sharp alertness that is a poem?   don't ask   just lift the point   and drive it hard into the smooth unyielding side of the stone   engrave song silhouette on pedestrian phrase   only a nick at first   strike again   small chips spit back venom   reluctant to be dug out of tangled scroll   rest now and look   shape crawls from the block   the chisel   placed here and tapped gently with the mallet reveals eyes occult deep with the miracle of sight   and here   just the smallest cut releases a ripple of fingers on white hand   persistent   i whittle and hew   then whittle again   the breast flutters with poem life   there is no stopping the shave of sharp margins   an ugly fissure   rough unlovely   becomes the gentle swell of thigh   a tiny crevice the arch of a foot   i turn back to her   holding the sculpted whelp   unsteady but born